Your Angels Called and Left a Message

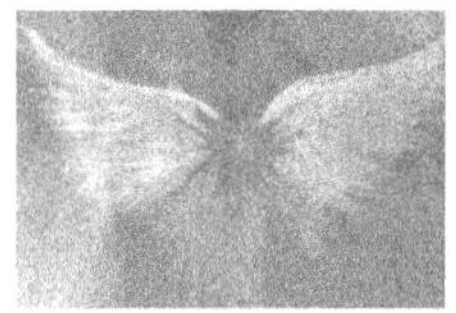

Divine Messages to Guide You to Happiness

Hemat Malak

Your Angels Called and Left a Message

Divine Messages to Guide You to Happiness

No content in this book is intended as a substitute for the medical advice of physicians. The reader should consult a physician in matters relating to his/her health. The intent of the author is to present information of a general nature to help you in your search for emotional and spiritual well-being. In the event you personally use any of the information in this book, the author and the publisher assume no responsibility for your actions.

ISBN: 978-0-9874508-0-7

Published in Australia

For the Divine

in each of us

What others are saying about

Your Angels Called and Left a Message

"This book by Hemat Malak is truly inspired from the Light. Be inspired by these angel Light messages, and transform to a higher vibration—this is a priceless gift for your soul."
—*Michele Blood, best-selling author and mystical teacher*

"Hemat, through her inspired words, helped me rediscover some forgotten pieces of me."
—*DR Rudina Thanasi (Europe)*

"The words in this book are of grace… I feel these words that are used come from pure Source."
—*William Scannell (Ireland)*

"These messages have awakened my inner self and connected to me true love and God. This book encourages you to listen to your higher self to increase your happiness, joy and peace in your life. I have not ever read a book like this with such profound and loving messages throughout. I read the messages over and over to get more meaning each time. They are such a blessing to read."
—*Gary Barwig (USA)*

"…I enjoyed it from my heart VERY MUCH. Thank you."
—*Zuzana Fancovicova (Europe)*

"...Thank you for what can only be called an experience of wisdom and truth."
—Susan Kowalczyk (USA)

"Hemat's messages from the angels energize me with delightful reminders of our beauty, connectedness, and how much we are loved. While reading the messages, I felt my spirit take flight with joy and delight. I highly recommend *Your Angels Called and Left a Message* to everyone wishing to soar and celebrate life!"
—Susanne Rothschild (USA)

"I like the GIVE part very much. I am believer in giving, as it brings lots of happiness; just to see a smile on someone's face means a lot. Very inspiring and uplifting, great work."
—Jaswinder Singh (UK)

"Simply go into the silence and know your true inner self will guide you to the perfect right message for YOU right NOW. Open the book, read the message, absorb it, then live it, and I promise you, your life will profoundly change in such a beautiful way. For each message is a pearl of Divine Light, and these are truly messages from the Divine."
—Zobeeda Madsen (Spain)

"When I read *Angels,* I immediately felt a peace and calm in my body. My breathing became more purposeful, and I could feel the depth of the words as I was drawing each breath. Thank you for your love, and blessings to you."
—Sabah Fakhoury (USA)

Foreword

I have had my own awakening and feel and see what is truth from on HIGH. This book by Hemat Malak is truly inspired from the Light.

I personally know Hemat, and her inspiration is real and pure. You can be uplifted by simply reading through any one of her what I call LIGHT POEMS. Be inspired by these angel Light messages, and transform to a higher vibration—this is a priceless gift for your soul.

The root of the word 'spirit' is the Latin *spirare,* to breathe. This is why many of her angel messages speak about STOPPING, BEING SILENT, BEING AWAKE, LISTENING and, yes, BREATHING. Whatever lives on the breath then must have its spiritual dimension—including all poems and, absolutely, these beautiful angel messages. I find all poets have tapped into a higher dimension; however, these messages are truly from on HIGH!

A useful exercise of soul would be to open any page at random a dozen times and find in each of the resulting pages its spiritual dimension; that will be a message you will KNOW is just for you.

Dive deeply into this book and drink and be refreshed.

This book can provide a rich and expansive opening that may lead one to a journey of self-discovery.

These messages resonate across time and space at the core of all human spirits. This will be a joy to give away as well as to keep. Listen as you read to the voice of wisdom, beauty, TRUTH and spiritual transcendence.

This collection lives up to its title, *Your Angels Called and Left a Message.*

—Michele Blood

Michele Blood is a best-selling author of over 90 books, audio programs and DVDs on self-discovery. Her most recent book was co-authored with Bob Proctor.

www.Musivation.com

www.MysticalSuccessClub.com

Contents

Acknowledgments

Bringing these messages to you in the form of a book has been possible only with much help.

My deepest gratitude goes to Michele Blood, who my angels led me to. Michele has mentored me, believed in me and breathed life into this book. She generously contributed the forward, her beautiful chapter, "The Practice of Meditation," the cover image and her invaluable assistance with every stage, including publication. Thank you, Michele, for your tireless work to raise consciousness and bring the love of the Divine to people's hearts. You are a true blessing.

To Treavor Rogers, thank you for your wonderful work with the formatting and preparation for publication. Your patience and compassion are appreciated. You are a treasure.

Thank you to all those who have taken the time to review the book and offered to share through testimonials. I appreciate every moment of your attention.

To my mother and sisters, thank you for tolerating my short phone calls and allowing my secretiveness so that this could come to fruition.

To my two precious children, Bianca and Leo, thank you for bringing joy into my life. I love you both with all of my heart.

I am so grateful for my life. I thank God for every moment and for His loving gift of angels.

"...we are never going to find the kingdom of God without poetry. We must let imagery and poetry have their way with us..."

~ Joel S. Goldsmith, author of "A Parenthesis in Eternity"

Introduction

Welcome to something beautiful that I believe will touch your heart.

You are the reason these messages have been written.

They are for you, and they have been written in love.

I use the words *in love* because they come not just from the emotion of love, but from the place—the position—of love. When I quiet my mind and go within, love is the place I find myself. And it is from that place that these messages come.

They are here for your happiness and to help strengthen your connection to the Divine.

I honour you and your beliefs. You may have a firm spiritual conviction, or a faith you live by, or maybe a feeling that there must be something *out there,* but you're not sure what. Or, you may doubt the existence of anything past this life.

Whoever you are, you are welcome, and I trust you will find value here.

So that you can understand the spirit in which this is written, these are some of my basic beliefs.

You are much more than your physical body and your senses. Your soul—or your higher self—is that part of you that you cannot see, which existed before your body and will continue once your body is gone.

You can think of it as existing in another 'layer' of life, and in that layer, you are connected to every other soul and to whatever you understand God to be.

The Divine, God, universal intelligence—these and many other words are used to try and describe the pure LOVE at the centre of everything.

The stronger your connection to this other layer, the more complete and happy you can be. Imagine never feeling alone, or unloved, or without purpose. The 'wholeness' of the self that combines both your physical presence and your spirit can give you this.

You don't need to study anything to connect with this beautiful, unseen layer of life. There is no need for any preparation or special skills. The only requirements are willingness and a request in your heart.

And for me, this is where angels come in.

My belief is that there are benevolent beings, angels, which are present amongst us. I believe they are a Divine gift to us, existing to assist us in our lives here.

Angels come to us from that higher realm of consciousness, beyond the human mind. They are from the realms of your soul—from eternity—and they work right here with you, right now.

From the moment I decided to connect with angels, my life improved.

Working as an accountant and being a mother, my feet are normally firmly planted on the ground. Being practical is one thing, but I had come to see life as difficult and annoying. I had gone through a separation, and the stress of working and raising two children (one with additional needs) had taken the sweetness out of life for me. I felt like an angry robot.

One day, I came across a video someone had made about angels. The idea of communicating with them seemed fanciful to me, but I tried it. What I felt was a wave of love that was so comforting that it brought me to tears.

I continued mentally speaking to my new friends, asking for help and being grateful. The drama seemed to slip out of my life and was replaced by a sweet sense of peace.

I now feel that I have constant companions who are wise and filled with so much love for me. It is such a beautiful feeling, and I am compelled to share it.

In this spirit, I ask angels for guidance that will help more people connect and live happier lives. These messages are the words that come.

They are as beautiful as poetry to me, so I have recorded them in the form of poems.

For me, they are messages from the angels, replies to my requests for guidance.

Am I certain that they are directly from angels? No, I don't experience concrete sights or sounds that would give that certainty.

Perhaps they are interactions with my higher self or from some source of knowledge bigger than my understanding.

What I do know for certain is that they are filled with wisdom that wasn't in my awareness and concepts I had not previously considered.

They are filled with a beautiful light, and I pray that it blesses you.

Read them with your mind open, and you will feel their truth.

I share them with you and, with all the love in my heart, pray that they will assist you to find peace, joy and your own beautiful connection with the Divine.

With love,
Hemat Malak

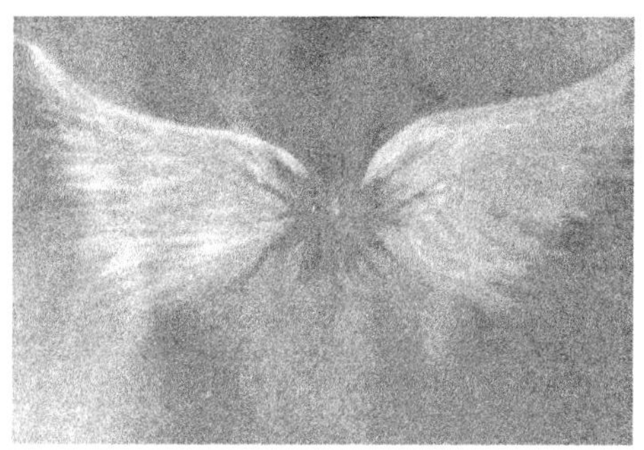

Welcome!

Welcome each soul you meet
like you have found a part of you again.
When you accept to see what's in between,
you will know the truth of this.
You are all connected, dear hearts.
You are one.
How wonderful when your paths cross
and you can know more and more
of yourself!
You truly are beautiful,
and you will feel the bliss of this beauty
when you recognise yourself
in each one.

Being Loved

Could you love
so much that you ache,
an implosion of love
to an unfathomable depth,
and then deeper
and more,
to eternity
and back again,
on a never-ending loop?
That is nothing.
You are loved infinitely
more than that.
Bask in it.
Even just feeling
the ripples at its very edge
wash over you
will change you forever.

Align Yourself

Align yourself with your heart.
It is the doorway to the richness
beyond this world.
Learn to be still and listen,
and you will feel your connection
to your true self.
Align yourself with each other.
Looking from above or below
gives a warped view.
Look your neighbour in the eye
as you stand together,
and you will feel your connection of love.
Align yourself with nature.
Learn to breathe.
Learn the real needs of your body.
As you purify yourself,
you will purify your world.
Align yourself with your path.
Recognise your talents.
Use them.
Walk your path,
and live your wonderful life!

Peace

To have peace in your life
is to have peace in the world.
Every expectation to conform,
for either you or another,
distances you from peace.
Allow.
Allow your lessons
and the lessons of each one,
and peace will flood back
into the beautiful space
you have made for it.

Hold Hands

Hold the hand of your angel.
It has been offered to you
since your first breath,
lovingly, patiently waiting
for you to accept it.
You are never alone
in this big world.
Pure love follows your every step.
When you throw your hands
to the heavens
in despair,
they are held with infinite love.
Close your fingers
around your angel's hand.
Feel the warm support
that will never leave you.
What a magnificent gift
you have received!

Oneness

Remember the Divine, dear one.
It is where you came from.
It birthed you,
and you are still connected to it,
as you always will be.
Let your memory come back.
Breathe the knowing back into yourself.
Breathe it into your heart.
You are one with all.
There is nothing to fear.
Relax.
Feel your heart swell with the love,
so much love.
It is inside you and all around you.
It *is* you.
All is well.

Join Humanity

Don't stand alone
and experience your life
as a lone blossom,
however beautiful.
Your beauty does not exist
without eyes to view it.
Look at the sea of blossoms
around you,
stretching as far as the ends of the earth,
each one as perfect as you.
Add your beauty.
Bloom together.
Glorify God in your united perfection.

Nourishment

Nourish your soul, dear ones.
Feed it and tend to it,
for it is you more than you know.
Sacrifice and suffering are often misunderstood.
To stand in suffering is not your strongest place.
You can serve and contribute as you are meant to,
in wholeness and in the fullness
of all this earth has to offer you.
Nourish yourself with its beauty
and wealth in all things.
To stand in suffering limits what you can give.
Break these limits
and enjoy the purity of abundance here
so that you may bring forth
greater and greater things.

Listening

Empty yourself to listen.
Whether you are listening to another
or to the Divine,
you will hear when there is a space
for the message.
Your mind races to predict,
to judge and correct,
to find meaning.
Listen like an empty page,
no expectation, no wish,
no awareness of yourself.
What you hear may astound you.

Quiet Inside

Keep a special place inside you quiet.
Let the busyness of your world
happen around you,
but shield your quiet place.
It is the place you can be to hear us
and know all that you seek.
It is where *you* really are.
Keep it always safe and pure, dear ones.
Protect it with your very soul.
Remember why you are here.
The contrasts of the world make it so easy
to fill days and days and days
with things that are nothing.
Your life will slip by so quickly, dear ones.
Keep a place where you can stand each day
and know what is.
It is your place of strength and peace and knowing.
Don't bury it under the nothingness.
It is too precious.
Here you stand as you read this.
Keep this place for yourself.

Beautiful Petal

Look around you
to your brothers and sisters,
holding hands to form
this intricate and perfect flower,
rooted in the earth,
nourished by her.
Feel the Sun on your face,
beautiful petal.
Its warmth is bliss.
Give it glory,
lift your head
and, as one,
offer your beauty
with joy!

Open the Door

There is knocking at the door
of your heart.
Listen.
Feel it.
Your whole house is shaking with it.
That dull, empty echo in your life—
it is not loneliness
or futility
or despair.
It is the knocking.
Open the door
and answer its call.
The Light will come
flooding into your home,
removing all traces
of your darkness.
Get up.
Open it now, dear one.

Understanding

Understanding is different for each one.
You, in the life you are living,
are one of a kind.
Not one other person on this earth
is just like you.
Know this.
Your understanding of all things
cannot be the same as any other's.
Please do not be harsh with your others
for their different understandings.
They have divine right to be as different as you,
and they cannot be any other way.
Together, each understanding can be combined
to bring you closer to the truth.
Alone, you only hold part of the picture.
Be open to the pieces that others hold,
and with joy, you can gaze upon it together.

Reply with Love

No matter what is said or done,
when you reply with love,
you change its path.
The way you may have known
was to let your mind and body react.
Stand outside with us,
and you can speak from the real you.
Here there is only love.
You can stop this physical world in its tracks
and have it follow you when you stand with us.
We see only beauty and perfection.
You too can understand this.
Step outside for a moment
and see with your inner eyes.
You will see the beauty, too,
and your love will flow effortlessly,
for it is who you are here.

Light

There is Light in each one of you.
It is the infinite Light of the heavens,
and it is inside you right now.
You will find it through your heart.
It will fill you with joy unimaginable
when you choose to notice it.
This is your very own Light
that connects you to humanity
and to all that is.
You are never alone
when you know it,
for you are part of something huge,
something marvellous.
Meet your Light
and transform.

Connection

Feel your connection with every other.
You are breathing the same air that fills you.
You are living the same life.
Move your awareness
from your lonely room inside.
Come out and look from the space
between you and another.
There your souls can meet,
like old friends,
embracing and filled with love.
How can you see anything
but perfection in this space?
You are one.
Love makes you whole again.

See the Wonder

Look deeply, lovingly
through the blindness
the familiar has cast on you.
The light in your child's eyes
is dazzling!
All the beauty under your shoes,
covered in your haste
to arrive,
is pure wonder.
All the lessons you speed past,
all the others
whose gaze you don't meet,
let everything nourish you
and inspire you
and teach you.
Blink and refocus
and see the wonder.

Let Love Fill You

Love is more than you can ever know.
Let it fill you,
and you shall be more than you are now.
Breathe it in.
Breathe it into your heart.
There it will touch your very soul,
and it will change you.
Everything in your life
can be healed with love.
Love yourself as we love you,
and our love for you is infinite!
You will glow with our love,
and you will become a beacon,
shining it throughout your world.

Strength

Are you trying to be strong,
to endure your life,
to carry another,
to push through the hardship and not feel the pain?
This strength is forced,
and it tires you.
There is an easier, softer
and stronger strength you can have.
Your soul and all the souls around you
have this strength.
It is the strength of the heavens,
and it is yours when you choose to stand in it.
Allow yourself to connect with your soul.
It is *you*.
Don't ignore yourself
and try to live
as this half-person any more.
Accept your divine self,
and you will *be* the strength you seek.

Having and Being

You can know this
about having and being.
They belong together,
lined up and in order.
Having follows your being,
not the reverse.
You will bring to you more of yourself.
You cannot have before you become.
This is time twisted.
There is a path that energy takes.
It will take this path
no matter how you struggle.
Why struggle when you could choose to flow?
You would be so much happier.
You are loved
through all your lessons.

Beauty

Appreciate beauty.
Surround yourself with it,
so that your senses sing.
Give yourself opportunities
to catch your breath
at the glory of beauty.
Flowers, art, music,
so many beauties can
surround you.
When your senses smile,
you lift your body into
another vibration,
higher than life and
closer to your soul.

Remember to Forget

Forget a little bit every day.
Forget how to judge,
forget how to criticise,
forget how to deny love.
The more you forget,
the more you will remember.
All the truly important
is just underneath.
More and more of it
will be revealed
as you forget the illusions.
Your essence is love,
pure, unbounded, endless love
waiting for you to remember it.
And when you do,
its Light will shine through you
and illuminate the world!

Smile

Smile with your body.
A smile is too beautiful
for your lips alone.
Smile your arms
around your beloveds.
Smile your outstretched hands
to all your others.
Smile your eyes,
and light them with eternity.
Smile your heart wide open
and allow the Divine
to pour into your world.

Angels

We talk today of ourselves.
We are here for you, dear ones.
Our purpose is to help you in this life you have.
You do not need to be any more than you are
to have our help.
Ask.
Ask us and receive all that we can gift you.
In fear, ask for our protection.
We will be swiftly at your side and all around you.
You need never be alone.
Ask for our help in anything,
anything at all.
We want so much to ease your path.
Your heart will hear us.
Let us walk your path with you,
clearing your way
and bringing you to all the goodness you seek.
You are loved and always will be.

Wealth

Wealth is good,
as all things are good
with right intention.
Do not cheapen wealth
by counting its pennies.
Wealth is fullness and generosity
and abundance in all good.
Be wealthy in love,
and feel its fullness in your heart.
Here you will know true wealth.
And, of course, it will spill over
into your reality,
and you will see it for what it is,
as the salt on your food.
Grow and feel joy in all things!

Believe

Believe the truth.
There is no need to search for it.
It is present in everything.
Believe the life in a flower
that is more than its biology.
Under the layers of learning,
the truth lies,
bright and waiting
for you to notice it.
You need to see to believe?
You can.
Use the eyes of your soul.
They see truth clearer than any
organic orbs in your head.
Belief is easy
when you allow the soul
to paint the beautiful truth
in your heart.

Stand in the Light

All darkness will vanish
when you stand in the Light.
Your worries, your fears, your judgements,
all can be healed in the Light.
Just ask and feel the Light of the heavens
surround you.
Stand in it,
breathe it in,
feel it fill your soul.
It is the Light of love,
and its warmth is wonderful.
Illuminate yourself,
and see your life glow!

Your Soul

You are more than you can see.
Honour yourself.
God has made you magnificent!
The limitations and imperfections
you may see in yourself
are just your learning.
Do not struggle against them.
Allow yourself to walk your path here,
straight and free.
The more aware you become
of the bigger you,
the you that is connected to all things,
the kinder you will be to your physical self.
Join yourself in your life here,
and see how bright it can be!

Doubt

With so many lives
alongside yours,
full of opinions
and beliefs
and lessons,
it is easy to become dizzy
and confused
and lose your sense of self.
Do your best to be part of the world
while you look out
from your safe room inside,
where you are perfect
and loved
and directed by the Divine.
Doubt cannot enter
a fortress of Light.

Decorate

Adorn your life
with beauty and color and music.
Make it wonderful
to come home to.
Fill your language
with words of love.
Light your eyes
with the sparkle
of your soul.
Paint joy
on every wall.
Smile your world beautiful.
Dress it with the finery
of the Divine.

Respect

Dear hearts, respect is value you bestow.
Give it generously,
for creation is perfect and unlimited.
It is a gift to others and to yourself.
To recognise the value around you
is to see, even in the shadows,
the perfection of what is.
There is a reason for everything to be
in the state that you find it.
What will you see?
Dress your eyes in respect,
and you will learn lessons to propel you
along your path.
Assume value, and you will see
more truth.

Allow Love

Allow yourself to love.
The hurts that you have imagined were love,
were not.
There is no space in love for hurt.
Love is here for you to take.
It is not made
of some earthly material
that you can fashion and fix.
It just is.
You can simply step into it,
and you will know its perfection.
And it will change you
back into yourself.
Then, any struggles you have had
with what you thought was love
will melt away.
And there is happiness.

Be an Instrument

Allow yourself
to be fashioned
into an instrument of love.
Let each lesson form you
and tune you
to resonate with the music
of the Divine.
Its notes are pure love,
vibrating the heavens
and the earth.
Allow yourself to be crafted
to perfection,
so that your unique
and beautiful sound
joins with the orchestra of Light,
echoing over eternity.

Fly

Escape your mind.
It holds you prisoner
as it tries to keep you safe.
Don't let its limitations
bind you any longer.
Your spirit wants to soar!
It wants you to FLY through this life,
dancing and turning
and floating softly through your lessons.
Quiet your mind
and release its tight grasp
on the little it knows.
Join your soul in the vastness
of Divine love.
YOU ARE MAGNIFICENT!
FLY!

Touch

You have energy in you that you may not see
but is as real as your body is.
Your touch can transmit this energy,
and it heals and loves and blesses.
Allow the purity of your energy
to flow to others in your touch.
Fill yourself with the love of the universe,
and your touch will comfort and nurture
those you share life with.
Gift this love to others.
All seek it and are comforted by it.
Do not allow anger into your touch.
It is for higher energies.
Your senses are a gift.
Heighten them and take care of them
and use them to serve others.

Ritual

Use ritual to assist you
to reach the Divine.
Ritual is a servant, not master.
It is the faint strokes on your page
to keep your words aligned.
Use it to rein in your mind,
to sit it down from its wandering.
Don't give your freedom
and your creativity
to be bound by ritual,
forcing you to follow
a path to nowhere.
It is just a support
as you climb
to reach for the Light.

Answers

Listen today to messages that are unspoken.
We speak to you in many ways,
and if you would look,
you would find messages right in front of you.
This is what you need to hear,
what you are waiting to know.
Open your heart, and you will see
the answers to your questions
right in front of you.
You are never alone, dear one.
There is no need for struggle and despair.
Know this and relax in our love.

Asking

Is fear or pride forbidding you to ask,
parading as your master?
They will cower at the feet of angels
when you ask for Divine help.
There is so much wisdom around you.
The answers to all your questions,
asked and unasked,
are here just outside your asking.
There is no need to keep struggling,
running circles around yourself,
blindly rushing nowhere.
All you need do is ask for your highest good
and then stop and listen.
In quiet, you will receive your answers,
and you will know their truth.

Encourage

Give this gift to others,
not just the others who are dear to you,
but all your others.
It takes nothing from you.
Gift it.
Encourage with your words,
your smile, your eyes, your heart.
Encourage when you see their distress,
their embarrassment, their awkwardness.
Encourage when others are mocking them.
Be a support whenever
you see someone stumble.
They are you.
Be kind to yourself.
Pick yourself up,
and send yourself on your way
with love at your back.

Struggle

Struggle is a sign.
It tells you
that you have wandered from your path.
Travelling along your true path feels easy,
like a leisurely stroll in the sun.
It is not frantic or rushed
or panicked or dark.
That is how lost feels.
When something in your life is not working,
is not flowing,
it is time to stop and find your way again.
Just stop and ask.
We can lead you back to flow.
Your lessons will still be there,
but you can learn in comfort and peace.
You will enjoy your life more
when you learn how to travel it.

Return

Return to your home.
You have been away so long.
What you've been searching for
is back where you started.
There's no need to travel any further.
Look inside
in your silence.
Alone with yourself, you will be home,
safe, warm, and loved.
Finally,
you find your place in the Light.

Helping Others

How noble the desire to assist another,
to soothe another's pain.
Be mindful that you may not know
what is needed.
The wrong medicine may harm, not heal.
You have a lifetime of experience,
but it is *your* lifetime.
Don't work alone.
Ask for Divine help,
ask angels,
ask for the perfect medicine
to be administered.
Your intention and request
will direct the energies of the heavens
to reach the one in need,
in the perfect form for them.
This is the magic that turns treatment
into healing.

Forgiving

It is not for you to forgive.
You live a life that is yours only,
and those around you live theirs.
The wrongs may be real, of course,
but forgiveness assumes
something amiss
in the path of another.
Your expectations are the mischief.
Understand that what is, is.
A heart filled with love
will not see a wrong directed at it.
The direction is in your eyes.
Look with your heart to see the truth,
and allow others to learn and follow their path.
Another's lessons are not arrows
aimed at you.
Your expectations can only give you pain.
Release them
and learn alongside each other.

Give Us Your Worries

Give us your worries.
Release them to us.
Your mind is sick of repeating them
to yourself.
As soon as you feel the discomfort,
pass it to us.
You can be so much happier this way.
Angels are your gift.
Accept it.
We can see where you are
and where you are going.
The perfect solutions are here.
Call on us, please,
so we can bring them to you.

Wonder

Wondering sees you learn,
not the learning of practice and rigidity,
but the learning of flow
and discovery and growth.
You can learn very quickly this way,
and it will not feel like work to you.
There is an easier path for everything here.
This path for learning starts with wonder.
Ask the question,
and let your mind stop for a moment
so the answers may be heard by you.
In quiet, you can hear.
Your growth will be much faster this way,
and your lessons easier.

Attention

Choose wisely what you give your attention to.
It will grow in your life.
Like a favoured plant you tend to and watch
and delight in as it grows,
you can grow love
or peace
or happiness in your life.
The magic of life is in everything.
You can choose what to plant.
Fill your attention so full of your wishes
that there is no room for anything else.

Revolution

It is time for a revolution,
a peaceful, beautiful, gentle revolution.
Turn away from the illusion of suffering
and see, instead, beauty.
See it and then, live it.
Dress yourself in beauty.
Oh, a revolution of beauty!
Your suffering can end now.
Revolt against it.
Peacefully take another stand.
You have power beyond belief.
Hold it now, and use it for your good
and the good of others.
Turn your back on the illusion you have been living,
and march into your new Light.
You will be filled with love's warmth,
and your heart will overflow with joy.
Try it.
Do it now.

Judgement

Judgement hurts you and hurts others.
It separates your souls.
Resist the choice to judge.
Allow others to be where they are
on their path,
and give the same courtesy to yourself.
The more you love and accept yourself,
the less judgement can reside in you.
You would not judge a tree for its shape
or a bird for its song.
The appearance and behaviour of others
are part of them in this moment.
All are where they need to be,
and the lessons for each one
are different.
Do not look with your eyes alone.
See others from your heart.
There is no room there for judgement
in the beauty of love.

Pity

Pity is a misdirection of your sorrow
for yourself.
Healing is possible for all.
And if healing is required,
the malady must first be there.
Don’t interrupt another's healing
before it starts.
Accept and, if you are called to,
assist.
But don’t waste precious attention,
yours and theirs,
on futile sorrow.
Your attention is better on your task.
Your own malady calls you
to come back and attend.

Reveal Yourself

Creation itself has birthed you.
You are perfection.
Share your beauty.
Bring it to the world.
Each one has their gifts.
They are not for you—
they are to give!
Bring them all to the party of life.
Don't leave them wrapped in the corner,
ribbons dressing you for display.
Tear away the illusion.
The wrapping is nothing.
Show your glory.
Enrich the world with it.

Protect Your Perfection

Hasten away from anything
that will rob your soul
of its Light.
The world has many distractions
that can lead you away.
Pure beauty is everywhere, too.
Focus your eyes so that you see
only what will nourish you
and grow you
and give you joy.
Protect your perfection
as you walk the world.
Your Light will cast away shadows
with every step.

Swim

Stroke after stroke,
find your rhythm.
Your body cutting through life,
moving forward gracefully
through its waves.
Keep stretching and drawing back
your measured strokes
through the cool waters.
It is so refreshing
and comforting,
enveloped by this ocean,
cupped in God's palm.

Meditate

The practice of meditation is an important one
for you here.
It will allow you to connect to your Light often,
and your connection will strengthen.
This will give you peace and center you
in your heart,
your place of Light.
You wonder why you need this Light?
It is food for your soul, which needs nourishment,
just as your body does.
Do not starve your soul
while you indulge your body.
That is dressing the shadow.
Quiet your mind for moments each day
without trying, without seeking.
Notice the stillness of nothing,
and see it flooded with Light,
a Light that washes over and through you
and fills you with love.
You are one with all.

Purpose

Do you know that you have a purpose?
Most definitely you do.
It is to be loved and to love,
to make this world you have entered
a better place for those here with you,
and, in doing so,
lift yourself to new heights.
That is why you have come
out of your comfort in perfection
and into this world of contrasts and colour
and pain and joy.
Each day is a gift you may have.
Accept it and cherish it,
and fill each moment
with your divine purpose.

Rest Your Mind

Rest your mind, dear ones.
It is so full, nothing more can enter.
In quiet, you can hear what you are longing for.
Your mind is bursting with busyness
that doesn't serve you.
Quiet it for moments whenever you can.
We are trying to answer you,
but you cannot hear us while you stand in the way.
Hush, dear hearts, hush so you can hear.
Your answers are waiting for you to let them in.
You will not forget the important.
There is no need to fear that you will lose something.
Clear a space
and feel the peace that will inspire you again.

Learning

Today you will learn something new
if you choose to be watchful
and see what is presented to you.
It may be an answer
to a question you have asked,
or to a challenge you are facing,
or simply something that will grow you.
Expect the learning to come to you
and be noticed,
and become part of
the ever-growing, ever-changing,
wonderful creation that is you.

Find Your Way

It can be difficult to find your way
in your busy world
with all its important illusions.
Standing too close will confuse you.
Step back a little.
Remove yourself for a moment
to give your eyes a chance to focus
and see the path at your feet.
As your eyes grow accustomed,
you will see that it glows.
Follow the Light,
and you can still walk through your world.
But you will step more surely,
and a smile will be on your lips.

Breathe

Allow your breath to be deep and life-giving.
Breathe not just the oxygen of the earth,
breathe in the Light that connects you to all.
Breathe it in and allow it to fill you.
Every cell of your body can breathe it in
and expand.
Glow yourself!
Shallow breath will tire you
and deny your soul its bliss.
Live a full life.
Fill yourself to your very brim
and then more.
You will rise like a balloon
nearing heaven.

Refill Yourself

Remember to stop for fuel.
You are not disposable.
Running until you are empty
may see you with too little strength
to fill yourself again.
Nourish yourself always, even as you travel.
There is inspiration to feed you everywhere!
Do not keep your head down
to finish using your current handful.
And it is only a handful,
even though it may feel like you hold much more.
Like your body,
you need to constantly feed your soul here.
It is easy to feel jaded and depleted
when you stop feeding yourself.
And it is easy to come back.
Just open your heart once more,
and all the deliciousness of life
will return to you!

Loneliness

Be alone
to cure your loneliness.
Searching for another
to complete you
is your searching
for yourself.
Half of you has been missing
to your attention,
and the joy you will know
when you meet *you*
will make you soar!
Be still, in your heart
and feel the Divine.
Love, like waves,
will wash away the illusion,
and you will stand united
in your solitude
with joy!

Open Your Heart

Open your heart to know
everything.
How loved you are,
what you must do,
why, what, when, how.
You have access to it all
in your heart.
It is not a learning,
or any form of getting.
You cannot get
what you already have.
Your connection to all
is through your heart.
What a gift you have!

Have You Finished?

Have you finished becoming?
You've learnt all you can,
done your job,
endured more than you should?
Even from here, you can start,
from this pretend finish line,
and find joy
to replace the bitterness.
Prune yourself back.
That tall, lonely stalk
pushed by every wind.
Come back down
and see beautiful new growth
fill you and strengthen you
and make you more
than you imagine possible.
Go inside and allow the Divine
to grow you again,
lush and full of joy.

Control

Be kind to yourself.
Your control has been there for a reason.
Gripping what you know
for fear of the chaos outside
is understood.
Just for a moment,
let go.
We will catch you.
What you think is chaos
has freedom
and flight
and flow.
You are in a river of life.
Trust us to protect you,
and let go.
Everything you wish for is here.
Let go and let the current of life
bring you to your wishes.

Give Your Gifts

Give your gifts freely.
You must not hold them for so long
that they wither and sour
and embitter you.
Do them justice.
It is the least you can do
to give thanks.
They have been fashioned and tailored
perfectly for you
to give.

Do You Fit?

Do you fit with your friends, your job, your family?
Do you fit with the images
you pretend are you?
Trying to fit where you are not is futile.
You can only fit where you stand now, as you.
When you allow yourself to just *be,*
in your wholeness and perfection,
then you will fit.
You will fit your *real* life,
not your life of illusions
and measurements and comparisons,
where there is no place for you to stand.
You will fit your perfect space,
and then you can show the true beauty of you.
You are each one of a kind, dear hearts.
You have specialness that is only yours.
And when you allow it to be, you will truly shine.
And you will fit
because you take your own place,
not the place of any other.

Cleanse

Cleanse yourself
to see your world new again.
Your jaded eyes can see
only the shadow of beauty.
Breathe in love and Light
until they spill from you.
Feel them illuminate
every dark corner.
Feel yourself glow!
Your eyes, dressed in love,
will see only beauty.
Look everywhere,
and you will be amazed!

Babies

Watch babies and learn
from their wisdom and purity.
Enjoy the wonder of this world as a baby does,
and it is wondrous!
Learn love without judgement
and honest communication.
See the Light in a baby.
It is your Light forgotten.
Remember and illuminate yourself again.
Everything is possible for you.
The world is at your feet, and you are perfection.
Have the future of possibilities as a baby does.
Have the newness of today as a baby does.
Accept help and give that blessing to someone
as a baby does.
Allow another to nurture you
so you can strengthen them.
It is a gift you can give if you choose to.
Try to forget what you know
so that all things become possible to you again.
This was always yours to have.
Remember it.

Refresh

Wash the sleep from your eyes
and refresh yourself.
The busyness and judgements
of the world can tarnish
your light.
Breathe the shadows away
in solitude.
Even when they hold you in place
because you are so needed
to do nothing,
you can be busy cleaning your room
inside.
Breathe the freshness back into it.
Open all the windows so that the Light
pours in
and out.
Refresh yourself,
bright and new again.

Pride

Pride does not serve you.
It holds you prisoner on your pedestal.
Life has lessons waiting for you,
waiting to show you
what you have come for.
Do not let pride take your lessons from you.
Be brave enough to climb down
and show yourself
and learn,
even in public.
What is public
but yourself anyhow?
Fear can disappear,
no matter how tangible it feels.
Just ask.
The greatest fears are no match to angels.
Ask and feel your fears dissolve,
and be yourself again,
visible and beautiful as you truly are.

Oh, Serious One

Relax your grip on this world
just a little,
just enough to see through
its illusions
of importance and necessity and haste,
busying yourself so full
of nothing
that your life slips through
your awareness.
Give just a little attention
to the Divine,
waiting quietly inside,
still and watching
for you to come back.
Unfurrow your brow
and lift your head from your desk
for a moment.

Air

Ponder air.
It will help you understand.
As you breathe it,
its timelessness enters you,
joining you
to all that is
and was
and will be.
Your next moment is new,
yet firmly held are you
in air's embrace,
as she holds all her children
and all of creation.
The lines of her palms,
deeply etched
with eternal wisdom and love,
are your illusion
of separation.

The Divine

Precious lamb,
you are loved eternally.
Your shepherd is one
with your skies and your meadows.
You are provided for
and watched tenderly
as you frolic
and grow.
All is well.
Enjoy your meadow.
Play as you wish.
Your needs will always be met.
Your shepherd sees all the lands.
You cannot be lost
to his gaze.
Follow the Light,
and you will always find your way
to softer ground.

Wake Up

Tired and weary see you seeking sleep.
Do you use every last piece every day,
so that you have nothing more to give
and nothing more to take?
Where are you in this?
Come back.
Come back and wake up.
Look after your body and its needs
so that the truly important
can have a chance to meet you.
Today will be gone so quickly.
Wake up and hold what you are given.
You cannot see your gifts
with weary, closed eyes.
They are dropping all around you.
Open your eyes as often as you can
every day,
and you will catch more and more.

Happiness

There is no need to look far to find happiness.
The burdens of the world
may have hidden it from you,
but it is here, right here for you.
However you have crafted your life,
no matter what darkness you are living,
there is a place of happiness tucked safely inside.
Close your eyes and, for a moment,
forget your worries.
Breathe. Breathe long and deep.
Be still.
There is a Light there inside you, in your very heart.
Here happiness will always be for you.
Enjoy it, let it warm and nourish you.
It will grow and course through your life
as you allow it.
Let the smile remain on your lips,
and feel the Light of happiness grow.
It will light your life,
bright and beautiful.

Attachment

Realise, dear one, that your attachments
hold you away from what you seek.
The intensity of your grip
creates a wall
between you and your desire.
Desperation cannot bring joy.
Every good thing is here for you.
With a light touch,
you can float through it,
and it will be part of your life,
gracefully, easily, joyfully.
Allow your good to come to you.
Allow life to flow and dance,
and like a leaf on a breeze,
you will gleefully live.

Remember This

You are loved!
You are loved exactly as you are.
Don't regard your lessons as your faults.
We see no faults—you are perfect!
When you cannot feel love
from the others around you,
this does not change your perfection.
Everyone here is learning.
Allow them their lessons, too.
Feel safe in your wholeness
and live your gift of life!

Healing

To heal others is noble.
Just your intention
can send healing light to another.
When you are centred in your heart,
standing in love,
it is your natural desire to heal.
Sending healing to the bodies and souls
of those around you
lifts you and heals your own soul.
You are all one, and you have the power
to lift the world to a higher place.
The energies of the world follow you
as you soar.
Send the healing light of love
to all those that cross your path,
and feel your heart swell with joy!

Safety

You need to be safe
when danger exists.
As easily as you breathe life
into danger,
you can breathe life into peace.
Choose your illusion.
Why not choose one
you will love?

Inspiration

Seek to be inspired,
and it will come to you.
Your inspiration may be
in the smallest thing.
Do not look far.
Focus under your nose!
Your days need not be grey
and filled with the sameness you tire of.
There is so much more to see
in the same gaze.
On exactly the same path,
your day can be filled with wonder
and beauty and happiness.
Seek to see the colour and dress yourself in it!
Wear it with your heart bursting with joy!
And your brightness will inspire others
and nourish them.

Your Turn

This is your turn to shine.
There is nothing and no one
you must wait for.
Your life is here right now
for you to live.
Each day, each moment is yours.
Unwrap them
and enjoy your precious gifts.
In your joy,
in the full living of your life,
you will grow the world around you
and make it beautiful.

Giving

Give without measurement
and with no record of debt.
Give where you are inspired to give.
Give attention, praise, money, love, good wishes,
understanding, belief, gratitude, admiration.
Give from your heart,
and you will unlock yourself.
You are not a sealed vessel.
If you lock yourself,
you are locked in with the little you have.
No more can enter.
Remove your walls
and flow with the abundance of this world.
As you grow in your giving,
your receiving will, of course, grow.
It is the nature of this place.

Purity

Purity is the absence of darkness,
the true essence of something.
As more Light enters your life,
you will know more purity.
Pure thought,
pure beauty,
pure love.
All are brightly illuminated.
Allow the Light
and feel cleansed
and renewed
and purified.
Glow as the heavens
shining on your world.

One

There is no you
or them
or it.
All is one.
Feel your connection,
and you will know
that there is no separation
between you and God.
And God is everyone
and everything.
Enjoy perfection
as you are living it.
Be joyful!

Laughter

Allow yourself to laugh!
Let go of your thoughts and worries
for just a moment
and let yourself just laugh.
Feel the release and freedom
when you succumb to happiness!
Are you holding your worries so close
that you fear to drop them
should you laugh?
Laugh anyway!
They may drop and disappear,
or they may soften
along with your heart.
Fill the air with your music
and let it bring happiness all around you.

Perfection

Do not wait for perfection.
You may not recognise its familiar face,
which you have passed so many times.
Perfection is everywhere and every time.
There is nothing, and there is no time
that is not perfection.
The perfect time to start is now.
The perfect time to speak is now.
There is no other time,
and there is no other state.
Live your life of perfection
now.

Live Your Life

Live this life you have.
Don't curse it and wish it were some other's life.
This is yours,
and everything you need is here for you.
Yes, you can change it and better it.
The next moment is a completely new one.
Choose whatever you wish for it.
Can you see the freedom and joy in that?
This is your gift.
If you could just know how much power you hold
in your choices,
life could not just happen to you anymore.
Here is the wheel right in front of you.
You can hold it. It's yours.
The control room you sit in is empty
but for you.
Go where you wish.
Everything is possible for you.
Live!

Concentration

How difficult it is
to keep the mind from wandering,
staggering and drunk
on life.
Sit him down
and busy him with another distraction
while you take over.
Love him, for he serves you well
when he is needed.
But when he is so inebriated
that you lose concentration
watching his antics,
you must step in.
Let him rest and sleep it off
while you remain awake
and aware,
communing with thc Divine.

Music

Music can fill your soul
with warmth and beauty.
There is music here
that has been divinely inspired.
Listen to it with your heart.
It will soothe and move you,
and fill you with love.
Serenade your soul!

Magic

Not sleight of hand, nor illusion,
there is *real* magic here for you.
You are filled with Divine Light,
and all things are possible for you.
Feel your connection with creation.
Close your eyes and see
Light, not darkness.
Magic is in that moment
when you sense how much you are loved.
You are one
with pure possibility.

Holiness

Holiness is not a trick you learn
to please a master,
not a way to stand,
or dress,
or direct your eyes
or anything that can be viewed.
It is a purity inside,
an emptiness of
the details of life,
leaving the pure love
at the centre of you
exposed.

Know These Things

You are no accident of life.
You are meant to be here now,
living this life of yours.
You are loved immensely,
exactly as you are.
You are a creation of the Divine,
and your essence is pure love.
All of life and existence
and eternity
are steeped in holy Light.
When you feel your connection
with this Light,
you will know joy.
All is well.

Companionship

How lovely to share your life with another!
Together, you are greater
than each one alone.
Love shared merges your paths,
and they dance and flow and intertwine.
Cherish your close connection with another.
Your love creates its own energy,
which lifts each one higher.
You are each beautiful,
and together,
you are pure joy!

Difference

Do you see the differences in others?
Different food,
different language,
different dress;
all serve to separate you.
Direct your sight to another's heart,
and the differences will vanish.
You are one,
and the illusion of separation
will disappear
in the warm light of love.
Open your heart
and allow it
to connect you again.

Running Out of Time

You have time, dear one,
to live your life.
There is no need to hurry.
You cannot beat time
by running through its carriages.
You can pass by your lessons
and come back around
to meet them again.
But is easier to learn them
the first time.
They have been lined up for you,
beautifully, lovingly,
with infinite wisdom.
Slow down.
Allow time to reveal
the jewels
crafted for you.

Humanity

Rejoice in the contrasts of all people.
Accept.
Allow.
Respect.
Each one is great.
Watch your world blossom
when each can stand strong
and fully offer their gifts.
You are good enough for God,
and so is each other one.
Trust the perfection of creation,
and allow God all His people.

Questions

Ask your questions to unlock your knowing.
Why sit in the lost confusion
before a question?
Learning follows asking,
and you are here to learn and love and grow.
Your life can move faster
as your lessons are learnt
when you ask.
Not understanding is no place to sit.
Keep moving.
The answers are just a little further
along your path.
Do not stop.
Wisdom is waiting for your questions.
Let it write the story of your life.

Angel Love

The love we have for you
is more vast than you can comprehend.
We watch you as you take each step, each breath.
Every pain, every joy—you are never alone,
not for a moment.
We wait with love outstretched
to catch you, to lead you,
to usher you back to your beautiful path of Light.
Be aware of us.
We are right here, so close to you.
Reach for us, ask, smile, know.
You will feel the warmth and the love.
Allow us into your heart,
where you will hear our loving guidance.
See your life blossom as God's divine love
grows in and through you.

Feel Us

You can feel us, dear ones.
You can feel the warmth of our Light.
And when you do,
you will want it to last forever.
Peace.
And love.
Everything else will melt away.
Allow yourself these moments
to regenerate you,
to fill you again.
Just ask.
Close your eyes and ask
that we be near enough to you
that you can feel our warm Light.
Please try this.
It takes nothing, and you will know.

Dance Life

Your world is alive with vibration.
Without the dead weight
of isolation around your ankles,
you can ride the waves
of its beautiful music.
As you open your heart
and accept your Divine Source,
your shackles release you
to dance life.
You will feel nature,
and it will move you.
As you meet another,
your souls can dance
unfettered.
Let the orchestra of life
lift you with its crescendo
into oneness with all.

Angel Light

We have Light we can share with you.
It is pure and flows from all that is.
It is love, and we glow with it.
This Light can nourish you
and make you whole again.
Just ask us, dear ones, and you will bathe in it, too,
renewing yourself and filling yourself with joy.
You will want to share it, too—how could you resist?
It is pure joy!
Ask to be filled with love's Light
and feel it as it fills every part of you.
Its warmth is wonderful.
It is our heartfelt wish for you to know this
and live with this gift.
Ask us, dear hearts.
All you need do is ask us.

Love, Here and There

Love is everything, dear one.
Know it well.
It is your key to a full life here.
Love everything,
yourself, others and this life you are living.
Love is always the answer
when you feel stuck or unsure.
Think a while when you are unhappy,
and you will see your way out
through the path of love.
It will be the easiest
and most joy-filled path.
As you practise love in this world,
become aware of the love
that flows in from beyond.
The Divine is filled to eternity
with love for you.
Let it teach you.
Breathe in its bliss.

Precious

You are precious to the Divine,
loved and cherished
as her child,
a mirror of your loving parent,
a beautiful creation of perfection.
How can you judge yourself
to be any less than wonderful
when you are cherished so by God?
Feel the Light of your heart fill you,
this glimmering jewel
that is the center of you.
Your value could never be measured,
child of perfection.
Know with joy
the exquisite beauty
of you.
Be dazzled by it!

Taking

Take what is yours in this world.
You may have been taught that taking is bad,
that it is higher to give.
We tell you that you cannot give fully
unless you also take.
There is flow in this world.
You will see it everywhere in nature,
the nature that you are part of here.
Allow yourself to flow with its movement
and see the blessings grow in your life.
Feel good to accept what you are given.
No apology is necessary.
You hold the same place as every other,
and you are as deserving as the rest.
Have the courage to lose your guilt
and take with joy and gratitude.
You will grow, and your giving will also grow.
Your life will be larger and more bountiful.
Allow it, and enjoy what is here for you.

Run Away

Yes, there is a time to run away.
Not to flee in fear—
we are here to protect you—
but to flee from influences
that do not serve you.
You have a path here.
Do not wander in the dark
when your easy path is lit
with the beautiful, warm Light of love.
You will know you are on it
when you feel its warmth.
And you will know
when you have stepped away.
Do not panic.
You are never far, and we are here to guide you.
Do not waste this life you wanted
by standing in the shadows.
It is your turn.
Come, walk here.

Others

Others are not them and those.
They are part of you and you of them.
Would you ridicule yourself
and cheat yourself
and judge yourself as inferior?
You are the same one!
You have forgotten to see
what's in between.
It is not space.
You are not separate.
Be kind to yourself,
all parts of you.
Yes, you have some madness
and strangeness and pain and confusion,
but your kindness and acceptance
can heal and strengthen
and make beautiful.
Look at others and see yourself.
You truly *are* beautiful!

Live

Do you live without thinking?
Are you too preoccupied to live?
Like an empty handful of food
that you don't remember eating,
your life can vanish from your awareness.
Be present.
Notice now.
See and be the fullness of this moment.
Give your best,
love, enjoy, smile,
look another in the eye,
breathe, know.
Open all your senses,
and make each of your moments count.
Life is wonderful
when you live it!

Be Gentle

Be gentle, dear ones.
Be gentle with each other,
and be gentle with yourself.
When you know your own kindness,
your heart will soften,
and its warmth will soothe others.
Harshness helps no one.
Allow yourself forgiveness.
There is no need to be right
to find your strength.
The more that love softens you,
the stronger you will be.
Give this gift to yourself,
and share it to strengthen the world.

Speaking

Allow your voice to be heard.
You have a place that is important here,
a place that only you can hold.
Do not hide behind another,
and do not hide from yourself
or from your life.
Ask for courage, and it will be given to you.
Speak what you believe,
and truth will grow your strength.
Your picture of life is unique,
and to speak what you believe enriches others.
Do not speak with pride or false modesty.
Allow your pure spirit to share with the world.
This will give you relief and even more courage.
There is no shame in what you know.
Use it to nurture others.
You are here to share and grow together.

Fear

Fear can take your breath away
and halt the flow of your life.
You do not need to carry anything alone.
Still your mind
and its frantic search for solutions.
There is a much easier way
that has always been here for you.
Ask us.
The moment that fear comes upon you,
call us, and we will lift it away.
Your solutions will come,
and your peace return.
God has gifted you angels.
Delight in us!

Wrap Yourself in Love

Wrap yourself against the cold.
Pull love closely around you
and snuggle into its bliss.
Nothing can cross its blanket
of Light.
Warm and comforted,
you are safe inside
as you were
before you entered this world.
You are forever connected
to the Divine.
Wrap yourself
and feel God's love again.

Stand to Serve

Offer your best
in service to others.
Stand tall and give
as sharing,
not as teaching,
nor as apology.
With your hands outstretched,
offer forward,
not up,
nor down.
All standing together,
all hands forward,
beautiful sharing of gifts.

Joy! Joy! Joy!

We dance for you in joy!
Love all that you are and have
and see your joy explode.
Allow it its hugeness!
Your faith in knowing
that only good can come to you
can give you and others great joy.
It is for you to take.
You will feel the Divine Light in this joy,
bright and beautiful, comforting
and filling you with its love.
Do everything you can to live in it.
You will touch those further and further away
as joy grows you.
Feel it lift you.
Your feet can feel the earth slip away!
The leap in your heart
will make hearts leap all around you.

Wonderful Life

Yes, dear heart, this is a wonderful life you have!
See it!
Your eyes will see if you will let them.
Stop the thinking that blinds you.
Just stop, and life will show you its wonder.
Relax.
You have so many needs and shoulds,
or so you think.
Your life does not need to look any certain way.
If you will just remove
all these layers of expectations
and just *be,*
you will finally see
all that is wonderful around you.

Where to Stand

Move your awareness
from your mind to your heart.
It is so much more beautiful there.
You will feel the peace you are seeking,
and your sight will be clearer.
View everything in your world
through your heart.
Let it speak for you.
You don't need to search
for how to be
or what to say
when you do this.
Your true self, in all your beauty,
is waiting there.
Be it.

Gratitude

Oh, how many ways gratitude can warm your heart!
You will find the smallest and the grandest
to be grateful for.
There is nothing in your life that you cannot,
with gentle thought,
see the gift in.
Praise and feel the blessings around you.
It will serve you and bring more to you.
Your light will shine brighter when you live in this,
and those around you will feel it too.
You will bring more and more and more
to the world
with this simple act.
See it for yourself.
Joy is in this part.
It is the happiness you have been searching for.
It's your turn here.
Don't waste it and let it slip away
without even seeing it.
The time will finish so, so quickly.
Enjoy it all!

Create

Bring something new to the world.
You are unique,
and you have been given something
to share.
Uncover it
and bring it forth,
glorious!
Don't think it is nothing.
Would you berate God
for His choice of gift?
Treasure it,
honour it,
and make this world brighter
as you share its beauty.

Sickness

When your body requires healing,
look to your spirit.
A healthy spirit has a healthy body.
Your spirit itself is one with perfection
and requires no healing.
The illness of spirit is really
the illness of connection.
Your connection can be healed
and strengthened
in any moment.
There is no need for consultation.
The healing salve of the universe
is love.
Fill yourself with love.
Become one with it.
Your body, infused with love,
cannot be anything
but perfection.

Renewal

You are always changing, always growing.
Just as the earth you see changes and cycles
and moves forward,
so do you.
Sometimes, what has been accepted by you
for so long
becomes uneasy and seems to no longer fit.
This is your growth.
Allow it to stretch you and discomfort you momentarily
until you find your new place.
Don't despair at your discomfort.
A slight change here or there
will see you stand firmly again.
Those around you are also changing and growing.
Let go of your expectations
so that you may all keep growing.
Do not hold another where they no longer are.
Allow the flow of life,
and your growth will feel like freedom,
not restriction.
There is no need to look behind you.
You have left that place.

It is gone.
Go where you are going.
Keep moving to newness
and greater experience of this life.
There is more for you,
and it is beautiful.

Knowing

In your physical world,
knowing wants proof.
Senses demand to be fed,
creating sights and sounds
to satisfy their needs.
Staying locked in your body
with its addictions
limits your proof
to the fodder of senses.
You cannot see far
with these eyes.
Knowing must come
outside your senses,
outside your body,
but inside your heart.
Go there
for certainty.

Flow

Allow yourself to flow through your life.
Let the goodness on your path meet you.
Are you stuck in the groove of what you know,
this trench you've dug
in the middle of nowhere?
It's not too late,
and you are not too deep.
Lift your head
and see the magnificence around you.
It's yours!
Just step out
and become one with it.
Rest your weary legs
and let life carry you to what you seek.
The path to your wishes
has been here all along.
Trust it.

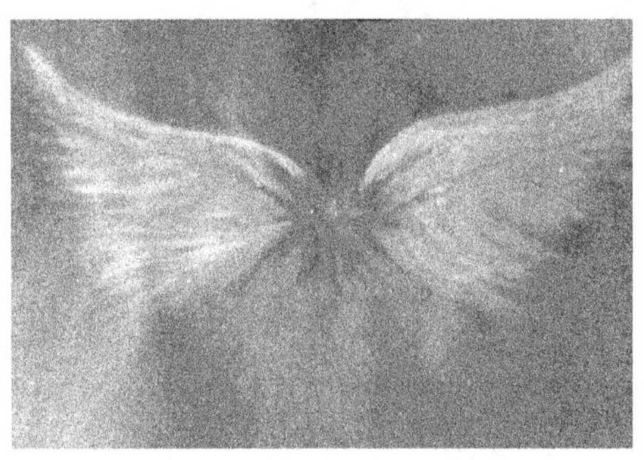

The Practice of Meditation

by Michele Blood

Hello again, beautiful reader. My dear friend, Hemat Malak, asked me to write a section for her readers who wish to go a little deeper into their spiritual practice. We are going to speak about *the practice of meditation!* Life can become more beautiful than any human dream. This chapter is not long in page number, but may it assist you in bringing more joy, power and peace into your heart and life.

Meditation with spiritual contemplation is beautiful, powerful and beyond words. It connects us to love, and love is the most creative and powerful thing in the world. Love is a *real* power and, it is pure, beautiful and can help you create a life of fulfilment and *real magic*. The practice of meditation connects us to this love and helps us connect to our soul/higher-self faster than any other method known. Of course, this is not only *our* opinion; this has been taught by every great master throughout history. However, *thinking* about meditating and *actually practicing* meditation are two very different things.

These instructions will help assist you if...

First, you have *never* meditated before or...

Second, if you *do* meditate but would like to bring the heat up in your practice and really feel its awesome power.

Meditation is a practice of making the mind still and connecting with our God-Self. Stillness is the mind's natural state. It is only when we become frustrated with the things that we desire or the things that we fear that we lose our natural state of peace and go down into lower states of mind. When our mind is engaged in meditation and mindfulness throughout the day, lower states of mind eventually lose their power over us.

So, how do we stay mindful?

Well, we...

- Contemplate beautiful truths, such as those that are in this beautiful book by Hemat
- Strive to be happy
- Feel grateful for every moment
- Be calm
- Do not judge
- Stay unattached to the *how*
- Bring power and focus into every action

We are not practicing meditation to become passive beings, no, no, no! We are practicing meditation and mindfulness because it makes us *much* stronger, resilient and confident individuals.

The combination of meditation with powerful focused action will allow our life projects to be realized and completed with great fulfilment and...SUCCESS! Our minds will no longer be focused on what we *do not want,* but instead will be focused with love on the task at hand, in the moment and with joy. When we work on a project with joy, magical powers of Light come in to assist. This

Holy Light, which is the source of all creation, blesses everyone. People will be more attracted to your work than *ever* before.

It is important to have *big goals* and *beautiful intentions* for our life. When we are drawn to "The Good Life," which is our Divine birth right, this is our Divine self saying, *"YES, you deserve this. Go for it."* God's duty is also our own duty; it is one and the same. However, if we have trouble focusing, things may never get completed to our satisfaction and then, we will have no fulfilment. We may eventually turn away from thoughts of "The Good Life" and have our goals turn into powerless *wishful thinking* experiences of frustration.

What if I am agnostic? Can meditation help me?

Even if you are agnostic, look at meditation as physicians do. It has been well documented that people who meditate regularly have lower blood pressure and, generally, are healthier, happier human beings. So, do it even if the word 'God' is not your thing. Put a smile on your face and be still. Before you sit down to meditate, do whatever you can to put yourself into a happy mindset.

Meditation will also make you more sensitive to your surroundings, and you will begin to desire to release some of *the stuff* from your environment, career and personal life. You will want more order and refinement. This is a *good* thing. An uncluttered life will awaken within you a very pure and simple view of Infinite Mind. A cluttered life will just keep you, well,... cluttered.

What we see and experience on the outside powerfully affects everything else in our lives. With disorder, we will just never get to what matters the most, *peace, freedom* and *Light*. We take our clutter with us everywhere we go. Going to a spa for the day will not release the clutter; even if it is taken from our vision, it will still be with us. Simply leaving doesn't change anything. We have to simplify our lives *and* our minds. We must focus on the inner self and less on our outer self. We need to spend time quietly working and letting our mind go beyond our work into The Infinite. This is true mindfulness.

Creating Your Own Space

Designate a special place/space where you live to meditate in your home. Clean this area *really* well, as this will release old energies. When we meditate, it is best to have clean energy. Buy a brand new mat on which to sit. Light a beautiful candle and some incense if you feel this will give a calming vibration to your mind. Create a little altar made of natural material, such as wood. All items, including your mat, *must* be brand new and, ***most importantly,*** everything in this space must only have been purchased by you and *be brand new,* as you do not wish to draw other energies and lines of attention into the meditation space. Fresh flowers or living green plants are also good.

If you do not live alone, ask your roommate or partner to please respect *your* special place. Do not allow anyone else to meditate on your mat. When meditating, more power and Light is brought into this space so that each time you meditate in *your space,* it will become easier, as you are using the Light that has already been created to flow through and expand.

Do not meditate in bed if you find it difficult to sleep afterwards, as meditation increases energy. Meditation is not meant to make you sleepy; it is a very focused practice that later gives you much energy and life-force. You will be increasing *life!*

Creating Intention through Contemplative Meditation

Contemplative meditation practice can eventually lead us to a moment of pure silence, where, at last, all thoughts have stopped. This exquisite silence is deeper than any ocean. This is when power, light and guidance come to us directly from Source. When this happens, it is no longer our own thoughts coming through us. We have become an instrument of God's own mind. Eternity speaks to us. This is truly the mystical way. Mysticism is simply God speaking to us, but, for this to happen, we must learn to be still and stop our thoughts.

Now, let's go into some instructions on how to proceed with this contemplative practice.

Intention

1) Open any page of Hemat's beautiful book and read the angel message. Read it again out loud slowly. Then...

2) Breathe in through your nose deeply, hold it and then exhale slowly through your mouth. Do this three times.

3) Now, we no longer focus on the words of the message; we just ask the Divine to allow you to be open to the truth of the message in your life. Then, we let go…

4) Now, continue into the silence until you feel peaceful and an *all is well* feeling. Continue now in the silence and allow God to speak *through you* as a feeling or small, still voice. Now let go…surrender…

At the end of your meditation, take a bow of gratitude and say, "Thank you, my soul, today is already a magical day."

This way, our day is governed and directed by our Divine Presence, not our human mind, which can be a trickster and sometimes will simply *not shut up*! So, begin with an intention to connect with God and contemplate the message you have read. Then, go into the silence for approximately 10-15 minutes. In total, this would take approximately 15 minutes. Of course, sit and meditate for longer if you can at this stage without your mind wandering too much. Remember, we cannot think of two things at the same time.

Music and Meditation

This world presently has over seven billion souls living on it, and this number is rising rapidly. So, of course, in this day and age it is *much* harder than it was in a time such as the ancient Egyptian era to meditate. Why? Because we have all of these other people's thoughts and lines of attention continually bombarding our sensitive psychic minds. This is where music can help and where the very cool, modern iPods come in handy. We have added a recommended listing of meditation music CDs from various artists at the end of this segment.

So what you do is…

1) Sit down on your meditation mat and *smile* before you begin, as this will help open your heart chakra. The intention is to bring in peace and joy. Now, feel gratitude. It must be sincere. We all must have someone or something we are grateful for or to. Bringing in this feeling of gratitude is vital, as this is love.

2) Now, breathe in through your nose deeply, hold it and then exhale slowly through your mouth. Do this three to five times, as this will help your mind to quiet down. Now, put on the music you have selected and listen. Let the waves of beautiful sounds fill your being. If your mind wanders, just keep going back to the music and be still.

3) After a few minutes, or one track, focus on your heart chakra and think of a word, like *oneness, harmony, bliss, peace* or *joy*. So, whenever the mind wanders, go back to the music for a few minutes, and then, back to your heart. Do this for fifteen minutes or longer until you feel still and peaceful, then simply let go.

4) After you have listened to two to four tracks of music and have felt at one with the music and at one with your heart, you will have achieved that feeling of peace, joy and unity with the universe. Next, bow, give thanks, get up and go about your day.

All beings are made of electrical currents, and our bodies are outlets of this energy. The chakras are like an electrical outlet strip, loosely aligned with our spine, which we can plug into. As electricity comes from the ether of the cosmos, once we awaken the Light within us by plugging into Eternity, we are then true extensions of the universe.

Please feel no impatience with yourself or frustration if your mind will not shut up, as after some practice this *does* work. It is still benefiting you, and, even if you do not feel it, *you are getting results.* If you follow this simple method, eventually, you will find that outside intruding thoughts will cease, and you will be able to sit quietly in a peaceful state with or without music. Have patience and be consistent. Remember that anything new takes practice. You would not expect to be able to play Mozart after your first piano lesson.

At first, do not attempt to do this for more than ten to fifteen minutes, unless you feel like it. You are doing this only for a conscious realization of your unity with Spirit or to make contact with God. We are not attempting to see "light" or to have "experiences." If they do come, great! But if we become too fascinated with these "experiences," we could lose sight of the main focus, which is to be in the silence, by making way too much of them. Keep it simple (KISS: Keep it Simple and Spiritual) and smile!

Each time you practice meditation, even if for only three minutes, you are adding more light and power of intention to your focus and more light to our world. It affects everything.

Before we go onto to the next suggested meditation, here are some suggested music CDs that hold beautiful music that will help *sweep* you into your infinite, beautiful inner self. Set your intentions high, and may God pour blessings of great increases of abundance and life to you today and always. Remember to smile and breathe.

Meditation Music Suggestions – Anything that you feel is beautiful, opens up your heart, you can feel at one with and does not have too much singing, unless it is choirs (Mozart, etc.)

Let's Get Metaphysical: www.EMusiVation.com

Lake Melva Meditation: www.YellowBell.com

Diane Arkenstone: Jewel in the Sun (iTunes)

Tangerine Dream: Seven Years in Tibet (iTunes)

David Arkenstone: Altantis (iTunes)

Mozart: (iTunes)

Mysteria: Chasing the Divine (iTunes)

Visualization Practice

Now, this is *not* a guided meditation, nor is it visualization. This is a different form of meditation, as now, we are going into our meditation not to get anything per say, but to only connect with the Divine Presence. This suggested practice is to help those who find it easier to visualize to experience the Divine Presence. We think using meditation music along with this suggestion may also help tremendously to get *in tune* with the peace, love and joy that *is* the Divine Presence.

1) Sit down on your meditation mat and quiet down your mind. Breathe in through your nose, doing your best to breathe in deeply through *both nostrils,* hold it and then release slowly by exhaling through your mouth. Do this three or four times. Think the thought of *peace, peace* with each intake of breath and with each exhale.

2) Now, imagine a vast ocean. This ocean has thousands of soft, beautiful waves that go on forever. Feel that you are one with this beautiful ocean. Visualize and *feel* that each wave in the ocean is softly moving over you and caressing you with Love and Light. Each wave is peace; each wave is joy and love. With each wave, you are feeling an increase of more and more joy.

3) Now, feel yourself sinking slowly into the ocean's depths where all is calm, peaceful and serene. After doing this for a while, allow feelings of joy, peace and love to enter *your heart.*

4) Now, as you go down deeper into the ocean's depths, imagine the waves have gone down with you and have transformed into soft, luminous, golden rings. See these beautiful soft, luminous, golden rings come down from above and softly encircle your whole body, one after another after another. These are waves of Light, and you are one with them. See these golden rings softy dissolve into your body and then fill your whole space with soft, golden, luminous Light. Such exquisite peace is now part of you, *as you.* After a while, let your mind go. Stop visualizing and just focus on your heart chakra and breathe. Continue this for as long as you wish. Your mind will return to this world when the peace and light have been absorbed.

Also, gazing at an object for the first half of your meditation practice helps tremendously. Choose a flower, a candle or a picture of your favourite deity and gently gaze at this object. Blink if you need to, but after 10 minutes or so, close your eyes and just *feel love* in your heart space.

The suggestions you have just read are to help you focus and become one with your spirit, your very own beautiful soul, which is your *guardian angel* of Light. So now, you may see what *real prayer* is. *Real prayer* is what we experience *after* we have set our intention, spoken our words and let go. The silence is where the *real magic* happens and what real prayer is.

May these suggestions help you bring in more Light, power and prosperity consciousness. It is our intention that each person who reads these words and practices is blessed and experiences an increase of all that is good in the world, especially the *real world* of Light.

If you are having a challenge with your meditation practice, do not give up. Allow these loving and all-wise words by the great soul, Paramahansa Yogananda, assist you…

"Your trouble with meditation is that you don't persevere long enough to get results. That is why you never know the power of a focused mind. If you let muddy water stand still for a long time, the mud will settle at the bottom, and the water will become clear. In meditation, when the mud of your restless thoughts begins to settle, the power of God begins to reflect in the clear waters of your consciousness."

Hemat and I wish you an increase of life, an increase of all good. Now, everyone, thank your soul by practicing the stillness and beauty of meditation and contemplating these beautiful, Divine messages. Things will change in your favour. Any fire can be rekindled in your career, in your personal relationships and in any area of your life!

This time, the excitement will be with more enthusiasm and passion than you ever experienced before. This is where the magic that is within you comes out to play. Rekindle that fire. Do not ever again take life for granted. Say to your inner magical self, *"No matter what is happening, I am going to trust this magic that is within me. I am going to believe in this magic and love."* Whatever you do, do it with enthusiasm and gratitude. Open your heart as you read Hemat's beautiful, Divine angel messages, and go out now and *live, sing it out! I am truly grateful for my life!*

May your life be filled with peace and joy, and may the Holy Light fill your consciousness with bliss.

In Love and Oneness,
Michele and Hemat

(Michele Blood's websites are www.MysticalSuccessClub.com and www.Musivation.com)

About the Author

Hemat Malak's journey to happiness began with her frustration at a life gone wrong.

A separation, two young children to raise alone (one with additional needs) and feeling stuck in suburbia all combined to lead her on a search that found her pleading with angels for help.

Through a Light awakening enabled by her connection with angels, she experienced a sense of the pure love at the core of existence. This changed her life.

From her home in Sydney, Australia, she now writes to assist others in finding their own connection to the Divine.

She continues to share angel messages on her website, http://angelheartlight.com.

www.ingramcontent.com/pod-product-compliance
Lightning Source LLC
LaVergne TN
LVHW010919110826
845149LV00013B/2428